DESPERATELY SEEKING BOWIE

IAN CASTELLO-CORTES

GINGKO PRESS

June '67
DAVID BOWIE

Nov '69
DAVID BOWIE

BEGINNINGS

The early years were frustratingly slow for David. He was doing all the right things, hanging out in all the right places, beginning to write songs that would later become classics. It just wasn't really happening for him. But he did meet, and marry very young, the incredibly driven Angella Barnett. She completely got the zeitgeist of early '60s London, and got completely behind David. How much of him making it was her responsibility is hard to fathom – she was later written out of the story after the divorce – but one can at least say that at this point they were a great team. They laid down the essential elements of Bowie's future success: his elemental talent for knocking out a great song and her ability to generate creative, shock-value energy. From bombed out Brixton in 1947, to his first hit single in 1969, was already a hell of a journey. David had gone through various bands, line-ups and a stream of small time gigs on the way.

The number of outfits is striking: The Konrads, The Hooker Brothers, Davie Jones and the King Bees, The Manish Boys, Davie Jones and The Lower Third, David Bowie and The Buzz, The Riot Squad, Feathers, David Bowie and Hutch, Hype, before he alighted on David Bowie, with and without The Spiders from Mars. The list is testament to his self-belief, incredible work ethic, staying power and several twists of fate. Without these, as Bowie reflected when he returned to Brixton for a visit towards the end of his life, it could all have been very different. Like many of his contemporaries, he could have ended up a middle-management accountant.

1

STANSFIELD ROAD

"This child has been on this Earth before."
Midwife who delivered David.

David Robert Jones was born in this house in Brixton on 8th January, 1947, to Haywood, a PR executive for children's charity Barnardos, and Peggy, a waitress. So far, so ordinary, but Haywood had invested, and lost, a sizeable inheritance in a theatre company and then a nightclub, before giving up on showbiz and getting a regular job. There was an entertainment gene in there somewhere and Haywood encouraged his lad's creativity. Peggy had a past. She already had a son – Terence – from a relationship with a wealthy Jewish furrier, Jack Rosenberg, and a daughter, Myra Ann, from a wartime romance, whom she gave up for adoption. Peggy's side of the family also had a history of mental illness. David grew up with Terry, his half-brother, in what was then a friendly neighbourhood of creative types, which had suffered disproportionate damage from Hitler's V1 and V2 bombs. He later remembered the fun he and his friends had, playing amongst the ruins of bombed-out houses.

WHERE?
40 STANSFIELD ROAD,
BRIXTON,
LONDON SW9.

❷
PLAISTOW GROVE

"It was George who was the singer, who did a great Elvis impression. Everyone reckoned he was going to be big." **Roger Bevan**

If Brixton was an unlikely place for genius to emerge, Bromley, a conventional, to the point of boredom, south London suburb, was even more so. This is where Haywood moved his family when he got a promotion at Barnardo's. It was here that David met lifelong friend George Underwood. They created a sort of band on a Scout trip to the Isle of Wight aged 11. George persuaded David to forget the grammar school and to go to the new Bromley Tech instead, with its strong connections to Bromley College of Art. Here David was taught by a brilliant, inspirational art master, Owen Frampton, father of future rock star Peter. After school David and his friends would hang out in the record department of Medhurst's, a Bromley department store, listening to the latest US imports. George was the one that everyone thought would become a rock star. An argument over a girl led to George punching David in the eye, permanently damaging his eyeball, and giving that eye the appearance of a different colour.

WHERE?
4 PLAISTOW GROVE,
BROMLEY,
KENT.

❸

THE MARQUEE

"If you wore clothes of a certain nature you automatically were a personality."
David Bowie

London's most happening club. David often caught the train up here, chasing language students and au pairs, absorbing the vibe. The trick, he said, was to try and look like Keith Relf from the Yardbirds. David had already started experimenting with his look, wearing flowing, lemon-yellow hair, and Robin Hood-style suede boots. He was also getting out there, singing with various bands – The Konrads, The Manish Boys and The Lower Third. He frequently played The Marquee, first in 1964, then every year till '69. But success was eluding him; his friends thought he was too much of a dilettante/ entertainer to really make it. But David was an amazing networker, with a hyper-keen instinct for publicity. A case in point was when he appeared on BBC TV in 1964, aged 17, to explain why he had founded 'The Society for the Prevention of Cruelty to Long-Haired Men'.

WHERE?
90 WARDOUR STREET,
SOHO,
LONDON W1.

THE LOWER THIRD

9

❹

FOXGROVE ROAD

"Would you like to come downstairs and sample a tincture of cannabis and have a cup of tea?" Mary Finnigan

David had a talent for floating in and out of situations. He was visiting his friends the Jacksons in Beckenham, strumming his guitar, when Mary Finnigan heard him from her garden and invited him down. They chatted, she asked if he would like to become her lodger, he moved in, they became lovers, he paid no rent. David had been trying to make it for six years, but it wasn't happening for him: he was broke. But it was here that he first played Mary *Space Oddity*. Unbeknown to Mary he was also simultaneously sleeping, up in London, with Calvin Mark Lee, a fascinating and very well networked Mercury Records A&R man, Lindsay Kemp, the revolutionary mime artist, Ken Pitt his third manager, and soon Calvin Mark Lee's hyper-energetic American girlfriend, Angela Barnett, aka Angie. Mary was relaxed when he later moved Angie into Foxgrove Road for a while as his 'official' girlfriend.

WHERE?
THE ORIGINAL 24 FOXGROVE ROAD WHERE MARY
AND BOWIE LIVED WAS KNOCKED DOWN AND A
BLOCK OF FLATS NOW OCCUPIES THE SITE; THIS
NEIGHBOURING HOUSE IS WHAT IT WOULD HAVE
LOOKED LIKE. BECKENHAM, SOUTH LONDON.

❺

THE ARTS LAB

"You can have the back room....
I'll make my money on drink sales."
Landlord of The Three Tuns pub.

David had the idea of running a folk club at a, back then, pretty run-down
Beckenham boozer, as he wasn't getting any gigs in London and as he
was completely broke. Mary Finnigan, a freelance journalist and brilliant
organiser, created what she called 'a mini Haight-Ashbury' in the back
room, and David wrote a fresh song every week. Entry was just five
shillings. For the first gig only 25 people turned up, but soon it was jam-
packed. Acts featured included The Strawbs, Rick Wakeman and Peter
Frampton. Mary and David then decided to run an arts lab (predictably
named the Beckenham Arts Lab) on Sundays, where psychedelic poster-
makers, puppeteers, painters, mime artists and writers performed, with
more music in the evenings. It turned into a real scene, particularly on
druggy warm summer evenings. David was riding the hippie wave.

WHERE?
BACK OF THE THREE TUNS PUB,
BECKENHAM HIGH STREET, BECKENHAM,
SOUTH LONDON.
NOW A BRANCH OF ZIZI'S PIZZA CHAIN.

12

❻

SPACE ODDITY

*"It's reputed to be one of the first, if not the
first, stereo singles."* **Rick Wakeman**

Space Oddity, with its very unusual harmonic structure, has been defined
as a song that emerged fully formed from David's subconscious mind.
David's manager, Ken Pitt, had sent it to Beatles producer George Martin,
asking if he wanted to produce; Martin wasn't impressed and said 'no'.
But inside Mercury, Calvin Mark Lee and a senior exec, Simon Hayes,
instantly saw its potential – they could tie it in with the most amazing
event of 1969 – the Apollo moon landing. They went into the studio in
a rush, and had pressed singles three weeks later. However, despite
being used as a backing track for the BBC broadcast of the landings, the
publicity around the release was screwed up, and it only made number 48
in the UK chart, before heading to oblivion. The Mercury guys in the US
had no interest in backing a song "about a guy who gets lost in space"
– wrong message. Then luck struck: a new manager in the UK, Olav
Wyper, loved it and put the whole Mercury promotions team behind it. It
re-emerged, Lazarus-like, and reached number 5. By January 1970, it had
sold 139,000 units. David wasn't yet fully launched, but, with his first hit,
he was on his way.

WHERE?
SEA OF TRANQUILITY,
THE MOON.

❼

HADDON HALL

"Hah! It was a crazy place. But one would expect that with all of us young artistic types living there." **Tony Visconti**

Angie had this incredible energy and talent for just making things happen. She understood how to work a scene and had a vague plan of becoming an actress. Being connected with Bowie wouldn't hurt. She found Haddon Hall, a sprawling Victorian mansion in south London as a suitable abode for them both: it was time, she decided, that they had a place of their own. The Hall had been inherited from its heirless owner by the gardener, who took some persuading to let them live there. But persuade him Angie did, and it became the perfect bohemian environment for Bowie to create. Bowie acquired a grand piano, and switched to that from composing on guitar. Angie and Bowie ran their open marriage from here: loads of sex with different partners and an atmosphere of real decadence. It was whilst at Haddon that their son Zowie was born. It was also at Haddon Hall that Bowie began to dream up his alter-ego, Ziggy Stardust.

WHERE?
240 SOUTHEND ROAD,
BECKENHAM,
SOUTH LONDON.
DEMOLISHED IN 1984.

Nov '70
THE MAN WHO SOLD
THE WORLD

Nov '71
HUNKY DORY

1970–1971

Space Oddity the single was a hit, but the album, initially titled *David Bowie* (later renamed *Space Oddity*), was a flop. Ken Pitt was fired and replaced by a lawyer, Tony Defries. Defries recognised Bowie's talent and potential and vowed to make him a star. He also drafted a 50%/50% contract, but one where Bowie did not have a share in the eventual management company (MainMan), and where Defries was paid his 50% share whole, whilst Bowie's was net of expenses (he found for instance, that he alone was covering the huge cost of tours). But Bowie was not focused on the fine print, but on getting ahead and becoming more than a one-hit wonder.

Encouraged by Angie, who loved anything outrageous, he started pushing his own gender-bending take on a nascent glam scene: in the 1970s this was still transgressive; it had a huge impact. Defries and Bowie were working brilliantly together, and the energy levels stepped up. His song writing became prolific and the spine of the first band that really worked for him – later known as the Spiders from Mars – was formed, with Mick Ronson, Woody Woodmansey and Trevor Bolder.

In '71 Bowie was back and forth across the Atlantic; in January he went on a US promotional tour, to East and West coasts; in June he played Glastonbury; in August he was at The Roundhouse in London to watch Warhol's play *Pork*. He released two albums that year, *The Man Who Sold the World* (April) followed by *Hunky Dory* (November).

Defries decided to go for a change of record company, from Mercury to RCA – the mega US company whose roster of artists included Elvis. Bowie was back in NYC in September to sign the RCA contract and whilst there he met Warhol at the Factory and Iggy Pop at Max's Kansas City. Then in November he began recording, in Trident Studios in London, the transformative *The Rise and Fall of Ziggy Stardust and the Spiders from Mars*. It was all coming together very fast.

❶

MR FISH

"Ravishing...disconcertingly reminiscent of Lauren Bacall." Rolling Stone **magazine on Bowie in his Mr Fish dress.**

The brilliant designer Michael Fish trained at Turnbull & Asser, the classic Jermyn Street outfitters, designing shirts, before opening his amazing, scene-changing boutique in Clifford Street, Mayfair. It was Angie in her impresario mode who, popping in to Mr Fish, first spotted a dress Fish created to be worn by men. She told David to try it on, and they walked out with two, which David used for his 1971 tour of the US. David also wore the dress for the cover of *The Man Who Sold The World*, pushing his gay/straight ambiguity to amazing – for the time – effect. That Mr Fish dress was something of a catalyst for the next transformative phase in Bowie's life: Ziggy.

WHERE?
CLIFFORD STREET,
MAYFAIR,
LONDON W1.

2

GREENWICH VILLAGE, NYC

"I couldn't believe the country could be so free, so intoxicating...It suddenly made Beckenham feel very small, very timid, very English." **David Bowie**

The '71 promotional tour to the US was a real eye opener for Bowie. He was blown away by the NYC scene around Warhol, heard a Velvet Underground album for the first time in Greenwich Village, and also realised he'd struck a chord with his Mr Fish dress and long hair, at a time when the transvestites in the Greenwich Village were hugely in fashion. This was the time, Bowie said, when the whole Ziggy thing really gelled, in particular the idea that Bowie would not only be his alter-ego on stage, but off it too. After eight years of trying to make it, it felt like something was starting to happen, and something big.

WHERE?
GREENWICH VILLAGE,
MANHATTAN,
NYC

❸
SUNSET STRIP, L.A.

"All the kids thought he looked like an old Hollywood film star, like Veronica Lake."
Rodney Bingenheimer, DJ

In February '71, Mercury were still notionally David's record company. They hired Rodney Bingenheimer, a local DJ, to chauffeur David around the L.A. leg of his promotional trip. Rodney took him up to parties in the Hollywood Hills, to Brentwood, to the valleys and introduced him to Marlon Brando, Elton John and Gene Vincent. His look – the hair, the floppy hats and the dresses, was a hit, just as it had been in New York. David hung out at Rodney's E Club, just by the Chateau Marmont on Sunset Strip. Stuff out of London was becoming very hip in L.A., and a year after Bowie's visit, and at his suggestion, Rodney opened a second club, English Disco, where in addition to Bowie they played T. Rex, Roxy Music, Suzi Quatro and The Sweet: "it was like a Bowie cathedral...they all came for the girls, the beer and the steak and kidney pies."

WHERE?
SUNSET STRIP,
WEST HOLLYWOOD,
LOS ANGELES,
CALIFORNIA.

4

GLASTONBURY

"At the time he wasn't on anyone's radar. We thought of him as an artist with just one hit."
Julien Temple

Glastonbury – then quaintly know as Glastonbury Fayre – was a slightly chaotic, relaxed affair in 1971: no fences, no tickets, haphazard timings, big celebrities just wandering around, and lots of hippy nakedness and sex. Bowie and Angie went down by train and then had to cross muddy fields from the small country station, with David wearing a three musketeers hat, Oxford bags, and absurdly unsuitable fine leather shoes. The big draw for the crowd on the Pyramid Stage was Traffic, who were late, so Bowie got bumped. He ended up playing at dawn and blew everyone's mind. As Julien Temple remembers, six thousand people were hypnotised by his performance. A hard-core group of fans had emerged, and the sense again that things were coming together.

WHERE?
GLASTONBURY,
SOMERSET,
WEST ENGLAND.

5

THE ROUNDHOUSE

"People were titillated as they were repulsed and disgusted by us."
Cherry Vanilla, groupie, star of *Pork*.

Andy Warhol's play *Pork*, featuring a lot of on-stage nudity, began a short run in NYC in May, before opening at London's Roundhouse to outrage (and great ticket sales) in August. Andy, in typically Warholian fashion, picked a groupie, Cherry Vanilla, for the title role. Leee (yes, he spelt it like that) Black Childers was the assistant director. According to Cherry, she and Leee saw themselves as 'Warhol's stars in London' and wanted to have as much fun, and sex with rock stars, as possible. Bowie was on their target list. Cherry, posing as a journalist, got it on with Bowie, and Bowie, who already admired Warhol, went to see the performance many times. Defries was opening MainMan in Manhattan, and needed a staff to run it. He needed execs who would get the cool and edginess of Bowie – hard to find. So he hit on a ruse: why not use the outrageous cast of *Pork* – Cherry, Leee, Jane County – to act at being execs? It worked brilliantly: all joined MainMan. To cap it all, Tony Zanetta, who played the Warhol part in *Pork*, became MainMan's President in the US.

WHERE?
ANDY WARHOL'S *PORK*,
AT THE ROUNDHOUSE IN LONDON.
ON THE BED IS CHERRY VANILLA;
WARHOL WAS PLAYED BY TONY ZANETTA.

❻

THE WARWICK HOTEL

"They were both extremely ambitious... It was kismet when they came together."
Tony Zanetta on Bowie and Tony Defries.

Convinced that Bowie had the talent to be a mega-star, and to make him hugely wealthy, Tony Defries aimed high from the get-go. He ditched Mercury Records and decided on RCA: nothing less than Elvis's record label would do for the man who would, he predicted, define the '70s. From now on David would have to act as though he was already a star, by being inaccessible and surrounded by flunkies. Defries himself adopted fur coats and always carried a big cigar. So when they arrived in NYC in September '71, they held court at The Warwick – where the Beatles always stayed when they were in town. The symbolism of the message to RCA was clear: the Beatles were the '60s, Bowie is the '70s: don't miss the opportunity. Dennis Katz, head of RCA A&R, was already hot to trot. He'd heard, and loved, the acetates of *Hunky Dory*. The deal was signed on 9th September, a huge coup for Defries, and proof of his strength as a deal-maker. The US was ready for take-off.

WHERE?
65 WEST 54TH STREET,
MANHATTAN,
NYC.

7

THE FACTORY

"The guy was just very quiet, like a lethal sort of Svengali figure."
David Bowie on Warhol.

The deal with RCA opened lots of doors, to lots of happenings and lots of parties. David was already slightly obsessed with Warhol and with what he was doing with the Velvet Underground. It was Tony Zanetta who took David to Andy Warhol's Factory (the first one, on 47th Street), to meet Andy, but it wasn't a success. Bowie was fascinated by Warhol and his ability to capture the zeitgeist and to cross over from music, to art, to celebrity, to pop culture. David, slightly embarrassingly, did a mime performance based on a pierrot pulling out his intestines. Andy just looked dead-pan. Even more crushingly when David played him *Andy Warhol* from *Hunky Dory*, Andy just came out with a completely flat, disinterested, noncommittal "Oh....yeah.....that's.....great..." Warhol's only positive comment was that he liked Bowie's shoes.

WHERE?
231 EAST 47TH STREET,
NEW YORK.

8

STUDIO 54

"Only the mafia have more money than Studio 54." **Steve Rubell, co-owner.**

It was Bianca Jagger who introduced Bowie to the most happening club in NYC, and soon the most famous club in the world. Started by Ian Schrager and Steve Rubbel in a converted theatre, every possible uber celebrity could be found there, plus a stack of wannabees, carefully vetted at the door by Rubbel. At the centre of the club, hanging over the dance floor, was a huge figure of the man-in-the-moon, with a large swinging spoon. When the spoon came to rest under his nose, the man-in-the-moon would light up. Endless lines of coke kept the party tripping, and back rooms hosted intimate, impromptu orgies. David, now established rock aristocracy, was a regular fixture, along with Andy Warhol, Mick Jagger, Ali McGraw, Michael Jackson, Steven Tyler, Margaux Hemmingway, Brooke Shields, Jack Nicholson, Diana Ross, Olivia Newton-John and Richard Gere… the list goes on. The Party ended in December 1979 – just pre-AIDS – when Rubbel and Schrager were indicted, and later imprisoned for tax evasion.

WHERE IS IT?
254 WEST 54TH ST,
BETWEEN 8TH AV AN BROADWAY, NYC.
NOW A THEATRE.

9

MAX'S KANSAS CITY

"Each night was different and each night was proclaimed the last good night of Max's for years – and of course it only got better and better." **Leee Childers**

After a dinner hosted by RCA on the day the contract was signed, Bowie went to the legendary club, Max's Kansas City at around 2am. Everyone used to hang there – Warhol and his entourage, the Velvet Underground, artists including Carl Andre, Dan Flavin, Robert Rauschenberg and Willem de Kooning, writers Allen Ginsberg and William S. Burroughs, and Patti Smith and her uber cool boyfriend, Robert Mapplethorpe. The back room was notorious, not just for its gigs, but for other goings on. At the time Debbie Harry waited tables. This was the first time David and Iggy Pop met and they spent ages talking. From that moment, and for the next twenty years, Iggy basically never really left Bowie's life. Bowie's subsequent regular presence at Max's, together with Marc Bolan and the New York Dolls established it for a while as a home base for the glam rock scene in NYC.

WHERE?
213 PARK AVENUE SOUTH,
NEW YORK,
USA.

JUNE '72
ZIGGY STARDUST

APR '73
ALADDIN SANE

OCT '73
PIN UPS

1972–1973

The foundations for the amazing *Ziggy Stardust* tour were laid down in the closing weeks of 1971. David was on a creative streak, composing a host of classic songs for the new album, including *Five Years*, *Rock and Roll Suicide* and *Suffragette City*. It was late in the day that the idea of *The Rise and Fall of Ziggy Stardust* was fixed, an almost prophetic statement of intent, as events would prove. A critical development was the creation of Bowie's new look, in which Angie, who instinctively pushed the gender-bending, had major input, and their inspired choice of clothes designer, Freddie Burretti. The new look was in part inspired by the thug costumes in Kubrick's movie *A Clockwork Orange*. The try-out show at Friars, Aylesbury was a triumph. What is striking about the tour is the sheer scale of it. It kicked off on February 10th '72, in Tolworth, Surrey. By September 7th, Bowie and The Spiders had performed 58 gigs across the UK. Between September 26th and December 3rd – the US leg – they added 26 gigs. They were back in the UK between 23rd December and 9th January '73, when they added a further 9 shows.

Back in the US in February, they added a further 16 shows by March 12th, before opening in Japan on April 7th, doing 9 shows by the 20th. After Bowie's interlude on the Trans-Siberian Express, they opened again at Earls Court in London on 12th May, with a further 62 shows across Britain before the last concert in Hammersmith on 3rd July '73. A total of 180 shows over 15 months, with two of those months spent travelling – David, who had developed a fear of flying, insisted on boats, trains and, in the US, buses. The UK dates were a triumph, as was the US East Coast. But in the mid-West, the South and in San Francisco and Seattle, attendance was poor and dates had to be cancelled, at huge cost. On balance, the tour was a success, despite often fractious tensions backstage. And in the middle of it all, David recorded *Aladdin Sane*. With its iconic cover, it went straight to Number 1 in the UK, toppling the Beatles' *Red and Blue*. Then Bowie brought Ziggy crashing down, with his dramatic announcement at the end of the final Hammersmith show.

❶

HEDDON STREET

"It was his fifth album, but it might as well have been his first. It seemed at the time that Ziggy appeared out of thin air, fully formed." **Rolling Stone** **magazine.**

The sessions for *The Rise and Fall of Ziggy Stardust and the Spiders from Mars* had begun in Trident Studios in November 1971 and were to finish in February 1972. In January, Brian Ward was commissioned to take the photos for the album cover. He chose a studio in Heddon Street, just off London's Regent Street. It was a chilly and damp evening, but Ward decided to end the session with a few random shots in the street. The band decided it was too miserable; Bowie, however, was persuaded to step outside. The result – a black and white amazingly atmospheric shot of Bowie, with his guitar, in a glitter suit, colourised by artist Terry Pastor – became one of the most memorable album covers ever. When they shot it, Bowie was still relatively unknown in the UK, and not at all in the US. No one could have predicted how Ziggy was about to take the music world by storm.

WHERE IS IT ?
HEDDON STREET,
MAYFAIR
LONDON.

ZIGGY STARDUST TOUR

Bowie's first global tour was a huge undertaking. He played a total of 186 nights (not including rehearsals) between February 1972 and July 1973 in the UK (3 legs), US (2 legs) and Japan. Interestingly there were no dates in mainland Europe. Bowie's fear of flying meant he travelled by ocean liner between the UK and US and the US and Japan. From Japan he took an ocean liner to Vladivostok before boarding the Trans-Siberian to Moscow.

SS Oronsay Los Angeles to Yokohama

QE2 from Southampton to New York

④
USA SECOND LEG
1972
Feb 4–Mar 12
16 dates, including
L.A., New York and
Philadelphia (7 shows).

②
USA FIRST LEG
1971
Sept 22–Dec 3
26 dates, including
New York, Chicago,
San Francisco,
L.A., Pittsburgh and
Philadelphia (5 shows).

1

UK FIRST LEG
1971
Feb 10–Sept 7
135 dates, including
London (9 shows),
Manchester, Bristol,
Oxford, Liverpool and
Sheffield.

3

UK SECOND LEG
1971–1972
Dec 23–Jan 9
9 dates, including
London, Manchester,
Newcastle, Glasgow and
Edinburgh.

Trans-Siberiann Express Vladivostok to Moscow

SS *Felix Dzerzhinsky*
Yokohama to Vladivostok

5

JAPAN
1972
Apr 7–18
9 dates including Tokyo,
Hiroshima, Kobe and
Osaka.

6

UK THIRD LEG
1972
May 3–July 3
62 dates, including 2
final shows at London
Hammersmith Odeon.

1

FRIARS, AYLESBURY

"That night just kick-started the '70s."
Kris Needs

Unlikely, but true, the market town of Aylesbury north-west of London had what was then considered to be one of the coolest clubs – which happened in the Borough Assemby Hall – on the circuit. Bowie liked to test new shows at Friars pre-tour, and it was here in September that Ziggy Stardust made his first appearance. Bowie had played Friars the previous October, with a set based on *Hunky Dory*, to a mostly folk crowd. This time, the arrival of Ziggy blew the crowd – which included Freddie Mercury and Roger Taylor (later of Queen) – away. It was all there that night – The Spiders From Mars had gelled, the clothes were amazing and that iconic haircut got its first outing. The audience went crazy. Defries's instincts about Bowie were bang-on. Bowie, in the form of Ziggy, was about to go global.

WHERE?
MARKET SQUARE,
AYLESBURY,
BUCKINGHAMSHIRE.

❷

QE2

" He came down to dinner the first night in one of his Ziggy outfits...everyone turns around and is literally coughing up their soup. " **George Underwood**

Bowie's fear of flying was not an affectation. He would do most things to advance his career – many said that his supposed bisexuality was also a convenient way, early on, of gaining influence with key people – but no one then was going to persuade him to fly. He'd had a premonition he'd be killed in a plane crash. He did, however, follow Defries's order that to be First Class you had to travel First Class, and invited his school friend George Underwood along (although George, not wishing to get into a hanger-on relationship with Bowie, paid his own way, which made the latter quite cross). By 1977 Bowie had overcome his aerophobia and resorted to private jets. There was one scare, on the Serious Moonlight Tour, in June 1983, when a first take-off en route to Berlin was aborted, only for the pilot to then seem to lose control mid-flight. The moment they landed, Bowie fired the pilot on the tarmac.

WHERE?
QUEEN ELIZABETH II,
SOUTHAMPTON TO NEW YORK.

3

CARNEGIE HALL

"A star has been born. I always wanted to write that in a review and now I can."
Lilian Roxon in *New York Daily News*.

Bowie had opened the first leg of the US *Ziggy* tour with huge success in Cleveland Ohio. The MainMan machine had gone into overdrive, getting Bowie played non-stop on local radio, and the 3,200-seat stadium was a sell-out. Tennessee followed similarly: 4,335 seat stadium, sold out. And then came the big one: Carnegie Hall, NYC. MainMan again proved brilliant at hyping the concert to the extent that it was seen as *the* gig to be at in 1972. Andy Warhol, Truman Capote and Anthony Perkins (*Psycho*) were all there. The show was a triumph. Bowie had conquered New York and in quick succession Boston, Chicago and Detroit. But in the South – in Kansas only 250 people turned up – it was harder work. It would take David three more years to really crack the US.

WHERE?
881 7TH AVENUE,
MANHATTAN,
NYC.

4

TOKYO IMPERIAL HOTEL

"Theatrically he is the most interesting performer ever in the pop music genre."
The Japan Times

Still fearful of flying, David travelled for the Japanese leg of his tour by ship, the SS *Oronsay*, from Long Beach to Yokohama. He rocked up to the uber-luxurious Imperial Hotel, notable not for its architecture (the owners in their wisdom demolished the previous structure by Frank Lloyd Wright), and whilst there, met again with fashion designer Kansai Yamamoto (the 'cat from Japan' mentioned in *Ziggy*), with a slew of new stage clothes. The nine dates on the tour were a triumph, but the trip also allowed David to detox a little from US excesses and to immerse himself in Japanese culture: Kabuki theatre (including its makeup techniques), moss gardens and Samurai traditions; Bowie became fascinated with the ultra right-wing novelist Yukio Mishima, who had committed *seppuku* in 1970.

WHERE?
HIBIYA,
TOKYO.

5

TRANS-SIBERIAN

"It was like a glimpse into another age, another world, and it made a very strong impression on me." **Bowie, on Siberia.**

If you want to avoid flying from Tokyo to London, how do you get there? Easy: 600 miles by boat to Vladivostok and then hop on the Trans-Siberian, only 6000 miles and seven nights to Moscow. The journey reflected Bowie's originality, curiosity and desire to steep himself in true alternative cultures; the seeds of shifting out of Ziggy probably started germinating during this journey. Bowie travelled with friend and backing singer Geoff MacCormack and Leee Black Childers. They spent three days in a very drab Soviet-era Moscow, where David's hair and 3-inch platforms attracted attention, before going on to Berlin, then militarised and divided into NATO and Soviet blocks. They visited the Berlin Wall, when the creative potential of Berlin's Cold War mood very probably lodged itself in David's mind for future use.

WHERE?
TRANS-SIBERIAN EXPRESS,
VLADIVOSTOK-MOSCOW,
USSR (NOW RUSSIA).

6

HAMMERSMITH ODEON

"Not only is this the last show of the tour, but it's the last show we'll ever do. Thank you." **David Bowie**

David had returned to London on 4th May after his trans-Siberian journey, for the third UK leg of the *Ziggy* tour. *Aladdin Sane* had reached Number 1 in the UK chart. He was at the height of his popularity. But then came his announcement at the end of the final gig on 3rd July '73. Its impact was huge, with the *Evening Standard* headlining "TEARS AS BOWIE BOWS OUT". The grand finale had been planned by Bowie a few days before. He told a reporter from *NME*: "I'm knocking it on the head after the final show...even the band don't know yet." But it wasn't Bowie who was bowing out, it was Bowie killing Ziggy and – pretty viciously – The Spiders, at the height of their success. This realisation that you had to destroy, with studied ruthlessness, to recreate, marked Bowie out as the cult, ultra self-possessed artist he was soon to turn into. The destruction only went so far; all the Ziggy costumes were preserved for posterity, later neatly archived in his home in Lausanne.

WHERE?
HAMMERSMITH ODEON,
HAMMERSMITH,
WEST LONDON.

MAY '74
DIAMOND DOGS

OCT '74
DAVID LIVE

MAR '75
YOUNG AMERICANS

1974–1975

In the UK, almost everything Bowie touched turned to gold. After the *Ziggy* tour, he recorded an album of covers, *Pin Ups*, which went straight to Number 1 in the UK. The US remained a big question: Bowie was connecting, but not to a big enough audience. The future needed to be thought about. In the meantime there was fun to be had. In London, the Bowies had moved to Oakley Street, Chelsea, which became a glossier and more decadent version of Haddon Hall. Early in 1974, Bowie started recording *Diamond Dogs*, in London and Hilversum. He was also reading voraciously, particularly soaking up stuff on German Expressionism. Defries was in New York, expanding the MainMan operation there.

In June '74, Bowie crossed the Atlantic on the SS *France* and kicked off the US *Diamond Dogs* tour, doing 35 shows by the end of July. This was more than a nip across to the States – Bowie had decided that to properly conquer the US he had to be based there. He also introduced a totally new Bowie – gone was any trace of glam, gone was the Ziggy haircut. In their place came a look inspired by 1940s Harlem: double-breasted suits, high waisted trousers with suspenders and a retro haircut. Bowie struck a particular chord in Philadelphia, where he played seven shows. There were signs that Bowie was starting to break through – the *Diamond Dogs* album made it to Number 5 in the US chart, and his October release *David Live*, reached Number 8. In the midst of this success however, David was becoming addicted to cocaine. People close to him began to notice a personality change.

Whether his cocaine addiction helped or hindered his creative process is open to endless conjecture. In some ways he was seeing very clearly. No sooner had the *Diamond Dogs* tour come to an end than David began working with Nile Rodgers in Philadelphia's Sigma Sound Studios. The result was *Young Americans*, released in March 1975. It was a complete reinvention, featuring a soul and funk vibe. A late addition to the album, *Fame*, was to be David's first US No 1. Bowie, finally, had cracked the States.

But behind the scenes there were problems. David discovered how one-sided MainMan's contract with him was; he was effectively an employee. He felt betrayed by Defries, who he had in part seen as a father figure. 1975 proved a strange year – Bowie retired into a somewhat paranoid cocaine cocoon in L.A., emerging however to star brilliantly in his first Hollywood movie: Nicolas Roeg's, *The Man Who Fell to Earth*.

1

OAKLEY STREET

"Bowie was more Don Juan than Dorian Gray." Hanif Kureishi in *The Guardian*

Mary Finnigan had complained that as soon as Ziggy started happening, the decadence at Haddon Hall went up several notches. With the success of the first tour Angie decided that they should move to Chelsea and ramp everything up on all levels. They took a house in Oakley Street, between Mick Jagger in Cheyne Walk and Amanda Lear in Glebe Place. The centrepiece was undoubtedly the fur-covered bed in the sitting room known as 'The Pit'. This was the stage for a series of amazing orgies, with David and Angie watching and then joining in. A regular was the London gangster (and allegedly one time lover of Princess Margaret), John Bindon, prized at The Pit for his very big (12", allegedly) penis, christened 'The Mighty Marrow' by Angie. But according to several friends, the first cracks in the Bowies' marriage were starting to appear. David relished the orgies, whilst Angie went along with them, and their open marriage, as very rock 'n' roll, but suffered fits of jealousy when she doubted David's attachment to her.

WHERE?
89 OAKLEY STREET,
CHELSEA,
LONDON SW3.

❷
CHARING CROSS ROAD

**"David gave me three clues: Power,
Nuremberg and Fritz Lang's Metropolis."**
Diamond Dogs tour set designer, Mark Ravitz.

Bowie *loved* bookshops, loved browsing and having his curiosity tweaked.
If he was into a new subject he had to know everything about it, and in
the 1970s books were the way. When London still had a strong bookshop
culture, the epicentre was the Charing Cross Road, between Trafalgar
Square and Oxford Street. It was Amanda Lear, who lived around the
corner to the Bowies in Glebe Place, and who famously modelled on the
cover of Roxy Music's *For Your Pleasure* (she also introduced Bowie to
Dali) who first awakened Bowie's interest in Fritz Lang after taking him to
see *Metropolis* on his 27th birthday. It was a revelation, and the following
day Bowie was scouring the Charing Cross Road bookshops, buying
up everything he could find on Lang. Soaking up German expressionist
cinema – and its references to the macabre, dreams and nightmares –
provided Bowie with a rich vein of inspiration for future stage shows.

WHERE?
EDGE OF CHINATOWN,
LONDON W1.

61

❸

MONTREAL FORUM

"The most original spectacle in rock I have ever seen." Melody Maker

The opening gig of Bowie's *Diamond Dogs* tour was also the first revelation of Bowie's new direction. The German expressionist set, inspired by the movie *The Cabinet of Dr Caligari*, involved an incredibly intricate staging with a bridge, a raised catwalk, the band hidden behind black drapes, sinister lighting and a cherry picker that allowed Bowie to be extended over the audience. Bowie appeared with a James Dean, blond hairstyle in a blue two-piece, 1940s-inspired suit. The message was clear: Ziggy is well and truly dead. The crowd were stunned and went wild. But there was no encore, no bow, just an announcement that "David Bowie has already left the auditorium." As many reviewers commented, this was a new phenomenon: Bowie didn't give rock concerts; his shows were rock theatre.

WHERE?
CABOT SQUARE,
MONTREAL.

❹

SIGMA SOUNDS

"I thought I had better make a hit record to cement myself over here."
David Bowie to *Melody Maker* US.

Sigma was the legendary recording studio where Bowie recorded most of *Young Americans*. It was here that The Three Degrees, The Stylistics and The Spinners recorded. It was Philly Soul to its core. When Bowie met brilliant Puerto Rican guitarist Carlos Alomar in early '74, he had already decided on the radical new direction his music would take. His many trips to the Apollo in Harlem, NYC, had fuelled his creative juices. Bowie began the recording sessions on August 8th, with Alomar. They worked at a hectic pace: helped by a constant supply of coke from Bowie's New York supplier, they laid down most of the tracks in a fortnight. The sessions were also characterised by arguments with his manager, Tony Defries. Defries hated the Philly sound, whilst Bowie was becoming conscious of how one-sided (towards Defries) his management contract was. The arguments were to end in a legal action by Bowie against Defries and his company, MainMan; the settlement, gallingly, kept Bowie tied to Defries until 1982.

WHERE?
212 NORTH 12TH STREET,
PHILADELPHIA,
PENNSYLVANIA.

❺

THE PIERRE

"It was a true authentic soul record; he had the formula 100 per cent."
Carlos Alomar

David had gone to New York, where he stayed in two suites at The Pierre, to mix *Young Americans* at Record Plant on West 44th Street. Lennon was working there too, and he and David not only hung out, but decided to collaborate. David had a song, *Footstompin*, which he and Carlos Alomar decided to record, but whilst the song worked live, it didn't in the studio. So David decided to cut it up, into more of a blues thing. Lennon had turned up at this point and played a little acoustic to it, adding, inadvertently, some strange breathing noises. When all the parts were laid down, Bowie said "It's done, it's finished." He went back to The Pierre, wrote the lyrics and next day did the vocal to what became *Fame*. It was a last minute addition to *Young Americans*, the album which finally broke Bowie in the US. *Fame*, in part an improvised fluke, went to Number 1 in the US singles charts. Three years after his first trip to the States Bowie had cracked it: he was now a mega star on both sides of the Atlantic.

WHERE?
2, EAST 61ST STREET,
OVERLOOKING CENTRAL PARK,
NEW YORK.

❻

DOHENY DRIVE

"When I wasn't hallucinating, I was sitting on the floor in the dark."
Bowie on his L.A. period.

Young Americans had been a triumph, but almost in parallel with his success, David's addiction to cocaine had reached stratospheric heights. After New York he decamped to L.A. (Angie stayed in London) and rented this rather ordinary house, with its kitsch Egyptian-themed decor. In it Bowie fed his somewhat paranoid state, with curtains drawn, black candles burning, and more coke. His diet consisted only of red and green peppers and milk. His weight collapsed to 7 stone. Like Howard Hughes, he started storing his urine in the fridge. This was the time when he developed his unhealthy interest in Goebbels, the Nazis and their supposed search for the Holy Grail. It was six months before he returned to the recording studio, this time for the brilliant, highly experimental *Station to Station*, which included one of Bowie's most iconic singles, *Golden Years*. The year ended with Bowie firing his new manager, Michael Lippman.

WHERE?
637 NORTH DOHENY DRIVE,
BEVERLY HILLS,
LOS ANGELES,
CALIFORNIA.

7

LAKE FENTON, NEW MEXICO

"David was very uptight about the sex scenes," Co-star Candy Clark, *The Telegraph.*

David stayed first at the Albuquerque Hilton, and then in a ranch-style rented house for the shooting of his first feature movie in June '75, Nic Roeg's *The Man Who Fell to Earth*. The movie's original backers had wanted Robert Redford. Then Roeg toyed with Peter O'Toole, before picking Bowie after a meeting in New York. Bowie's spaced-out, ultra-skinny condition may have helped, but one condition of Roeg's was that he wouldn't use whilst on set. Even if he relapsed a few times, Bowie benefited from being away from L.A. He gained some weight, and chilled out by painting in his rental bungalow in the afternoons. A condition of Bowie's had been that he could pick his own wardrobe and haircuts; these were to form the basis of his next alter-ego, The Thin White Duke.

WHERE?
LAKE FENTON,
JEMEZ SPRINGS,
SAN YSIDRO,
NEW MEXICO.

JAN '76
STATION TO STATION

JAN '77
LOW

OCT '77
HEROES

SEPT '78
STAGE

MAY '79
LODGER

1976–1979

It was at the end of the *Station to Station* tour, in March '76, that Bowie decided that the time had come to leave drug-addled L.A. to attempt a detox in Europe. David and Angie had already thought that a move to Switzerland might make sense, given Bowie's potential tax exposure in L.A. The idea – not discussed with Angie – of a parallel move to Berlin came after Bowie met Christopher Isherwood in San Francisco at an aftershow party on the *Station to Station* tour, in March '76. Iggy would come along for the ride: easier to detox with two. Bowie, always looking for re-invention, had also developed a fascination with Krautrock, in particular the work of Kraftwerk and Neu! Whilst Angie house-hunted, Bowie and Iggy made plans to record at Chateau d'Hérouville; Iggy's brilliant *The Idiot*, full of Bowie-penned songs, was the result. By August '76 Bowie and Iggy were installed in the Schöneberg neighbourhood of Berlin, before returning to Hérouville in September for work on *Low*. Bowie brought in the brilliant Brian Eno to collaborate on the album. The result, an inspired, original piece of work, which was suffused with the disjointed spirit of Soviet-era West Berlin, was described by Defries as 'a piece of crap'; RCA, in their wisdom, also hated it. It still reached

Number 2 in the UK charts, with no promotion. Perversely Bowie then set to work on another Iggy album, *Lust for Life*, and proceeded to tour it. Summer 1977 would see Bowie working on *Heroes*, its cover track possibly his greatest song. That Christmas was the last he spent with Angie. March 1978 saw Bowie back in the US, opening the *Stage* (also known as *Isolar II*) tour, his biggest to date, supporting his live album. In September, counter-intuitively, he was in Switzerland, working on *Lodger* at Mountain Studios, Montreux. Released in May '79, it completed what became known as The Berlin Trilogy, despite only *Heroes* being recorded there. *Lodger* reached Number 5 in the UK, and Number 20 in the US, not stratospheric, but respectable. Perhaps as importantly, Bowie was emerging as a sort of inspirational guru to much of post-punk New Wave. Joy Division were originally going to call themselves Warszawa, after one of the tracks on *Low*, and The Human League, Ultravox and OMD would also cite the album as a major influence.

1

HELSINKI

"As I see it, I am the only alternative for the premier of England. I believe England could benefit from a Fascist leader." David Bowie

Bowie spent the tail end of 1975 working on *Station to Station*, releasing it in January '76. It proved his biggest album success to date in the US, reaching Number 3. In February, David began to tour the album. He opened in North America, featuring his latest persona, The Thin White Duke, with a less-is-more aesthetic to the staging. Then, for the first time, he played continental Europe. This really was unexplored turf for Bowie. Dates included Munich, Düsseldorf, Berlin, Hamburg, Frankfurt and Zürich, followed by Helsinki and Scandinavia. This was the time that David was making deliberately provocative, right-wing statements to the press, enjoying their power to shock. His look seemed to fit – leather trench coats, Weimar-era hair, vintage Mercedes limos. After Helsinki, the next stop was Stockholm, where Bowie opened up with the infamous quote above. It was all tongue-in-cheek, and very predictably caused the furore he intended.

WHERE?
UKK HALL,
HELSINKI.

❷

CLOS DES MÉSANGES

"I can't write in a peaceful atmosphere at all....I need the terror, whatever it is."
David Bowie

Nothing could be less rock 'n' roll, than Clos des Mésanges, the luxurious chalet that Angie Bowie found for the couple, in the wealthy, smug village of Blonay, just above Lake Geneva. Angie was returning to problem-solving on a very practical level for Bowie. Now that he was pulling free from MainMan, and planning to take control of his finances, and with punitive taxation in the UK and California, it made perfect sense to live in tax-friendly Switzerland. Angie arranged everything with the tricky Swiss authorities, no mean feat. The house would be hers and David's first marital home, also allowing Zowie a happy, secure base. And it was comfortable, with a caretaker's lodge and seven acres, allowing some privacy. Angie may have hoped that with David committing to detoxing, their marriage could repair. It wasn't to be. David arrived in Switzerland, took one look at the house and ran off to Berlin. He did spend Christmas '77 here, the last one the Bowies spent together as a family.

WHERE?
CHEMIN DE SAINTE-CROIX 18,
BLONAY.

❸

155 HAUPTSTRASSE

"I felt joy of life and a great feeling of release and healing." Bowie, in *Uncut*

The decision to return to Europe was for Bowie one of survival: he had to kick his addiction, and part of that was getting away from his dealers. He decided to escape the L.A. scene with Iggy Pop. Coco Schwab, his personal assistant, who was also gaining power over access to Bowie now that his manager was fired, found a modest flat for David and Iggy to share in the lower-middle class district of Schöneberg. She painted the walls white and ordered blank canvases and oils so David could pursue his painting. David loved his anonymity in Berlin. He could walk or cycle the streets on his Raleigh with everyone disinterested. He could think, create, paint and compose. He could soak up German expressionism at the Brücke museum, or trawl West Berlin's many antique shops. In the evening he could hang at his favourite restaurant, Exile. His coke-induced psychosis started fading.

WHERE?
155 HAUPTSTRASSE,
SCHÖNEBERG,
WEST BERLIN.

4

CHATEAU D'HEROUVILLE

"There was certainly some strange energy in that Chateau." Tony Visconti

The charming Chateau, an hour from Paris and once inhabited by Chopin and his mistress George Sand, and painted by Van Gogh, was turned into a residential recording studio by Oscar-nominated composer Michel Magne (*Gigot, Barbarella*) in 1969. Word soon spread about its brilliant acoustics. Pink Floyd and Elton John recorded at Hérouville (including *Honky Chateau* – named after the house) before David recorded *Pin Ups* here in 1973. This time he and Iggy arrived from Switzerland, after a spot of flat-hunting in Berlin. Zowie joined them at some point, looked after by Marion Skene. Here David set to work on Iggy's album *The Idiot*, penning the classics *China Girl* and *Nightclubbing*, and then in September on the brilliant *Low*, which, with David's prodigious work-rate, was released in January 1977.

WHERE?
RUE GEORGES DUHAMEL,
HÉROUVILLE.

67. HÉROUVILLE (S.-&-O.) — Monument du XVIᵉ siècle

❺

CHEZ ROMY HAAG

"The atmosphere was...very undeground, trashy, kitschy...Like an Andy Warhol aesthetic." **Romy Haag**

Berlin's decadent cabaret club culture was thriving in the bizarre conditions of the divided cold war city. Local celebrity Romy Haag (born Edouard Frans Verbaarsschott), was a well-known Dutch transsexual who started her Berlin disco club in 1974, aged just 23. Bowie started dating her shortly after his affair with Ava Cherry ended, and loved the fact he could pop round to her club after a hard day's work recording *Lodger* at Hansa Studios. This was a period when Bowie was channelling Isherwood and the mood of *Cabaret*. Always the magpie, Bowie used one of Haag's signature routines as inspiration for the video to *Boys Keep Swinging*, which caused a storm when released in the UK, with its imagery of triplicate Bowie drag queens tearing whigs off their heads and smearing lipstick across their faces.

WHERE?
WELSERSTRASSE,
SCHÖNEBERG.

6

HANSA STUDIOS BY THE WALL

"I, I can remember, standing by the Wall, and the guns, shot above our heads...."
Lyric, from *Heroes*.

Right by the Berlin Wall, on a flattened piece of wasteland – "clearly an ex-war zone", as Visconti put it – was Hansa Studios. It was an eerie, alchemic place, where the gun turrets, barbed wire and East German armed guards patrolling the Wall could clearly be seen from the studio windows. This was a sharp contrast after the sybaritic Chateau Hérouville, and it was here that Bowie began work, first as producer of Iggy's *The Idiot*, and then, with Brian Eno and Tony Visconti, on his next, *Heroes*. The spirit of the place seeped into both records and, in the case of *Heroes*, into the lyrics. Bowie released *Low* (January '77) and *Heroes* (October '77) in quick succession. His record company, RCA, who really wanted a *Young Americans II*, found both incomprehensible, and they were equally puzzled when Bowie opted to tour with Iggy to promote *The Idiot*, rather than promoting his own releases.

WHERE?
KÖTHENER STRASSE 38,
KREUZBERG,
WEST BERLIN.

SEPT '80
SCARY MONSTERS

APR '83
LET'S DANCE

OCT '83
ZIGGY THE MOTION
PICTURE

SEPT '84
TONIGHT

APR '87
NEVER LET ME
DOWN

1980–1989

1980 would turn out to be a pivotal year for Bowie. His divorce from Angie was finalised (she got a modest settlement of US$700,000) he began work on *Scary Monsters* and created the brilliant, ground-breaking video to *Ashes to Ashes*. He wrote and recorded *Under Pressure* with Queen, which reached Number 1 in the UK. In July he took on his first theatre role, in *The Elephant Man*, to great reviews. Then the mood changed when John Lennon was murdered outside his apartment building on 8th December. As well as the shock of losing a friend and collaborator, there were intimations of mortality. "It was almost like a warning", he said at the time. David began spending time in Switzerland, enjoying some seclusion, and more time with Zowie, until he sent him off to boarding school (Gordonstoun in Scotland, a surprisingly conservative, right-wing establishment choice). Musically, Bowie was lying low, waiting for 1982, when new work would be free of MainMan's control. But he was busy with other projects. There was a bizarre TV production of *Baal*, the Brecht play, and two movies. *The Hunger*, an erotic horror, was Tony Scott's first foray into film, starring Catherine Deneuve and Susan Sarandon, with whom Bowie had an affair. *Merry*

MAY '89
TIN MACHINE

Christmas Mr Lawrence, directed by Nagisa Oshima (*In the Realm of the Senses*) was, despite poor box office, a brilliant movie set in a Japanese prisoner of war camp. Once freed of MainMan, Bowie exceeded all expectations with *Let's Dance*, produced by the legendary Nile Rodgers. It went on to become his biggest US hit. Then in 1983 came his biggest tour, The Serious Moonlight Tour. Playing in huge stadiums in 16 countries, this Bowie show was seen by 2.5 million. 1984 proved a quiet year, with the release of the disappointing album *Tonight*, whilst '85 was marked by another movie flop – *Absolute Beginners*. The year was also marked by the tragic suicide of his half-brother Terry, but also a triumphant part in Live Aid at Wembley. Another mega tour – The Glass Spider Tour – soaked up much of '86 and '87. Creatively Bowie had lost some spark. Both the tour and his next album *Never Let Me Down* (released '87) got rotten reviews. Bowie's response, in '88 was to start a new band, Tin Machine, where, ludicrously, he imagined he would be viewed as one of four rather than the global figure he had become. Stripped down, with a grunge metal sound, the band released its first album in May 1989, to mixed reviews.

❶

PETT LEVEL

"Ashes to ashes, funk to funky, We know Major Tom's a junkie"
Ashes to Ashes lyric.

The slightly bleak beach at Pett Level in Sussex was among the unlikely settings for Bowie's stunning video for *Ashes to Ashes*. Bowie, in a pierrot costume, more made-up than since Ziggy, was portrayed walking the beach in front of a bulldozer, with four extras recruited from Steve Strange's Blitz club in London. The surrealism of the video, then at $500,000 the most expensive ever made, mixed with nostalgia (he is shown at one point walking with a charming granny) and the inclusion of the Blitz kids, showed Bowie reclaiming glam's visual iconography, and placing himself at the centre of the new romantic movement, which was on the verge of breaking into the mainstream. Amazingly innovative then, it is still a haunting piece of visual artistry. In the process Bowie was showing that new acts inspired by his early work, such as Gary Numan, could never hope to reach the standards set by The Master.

WHERE?
PETT LEVEL,
NEAR HASTINGS,
EAST SUSSEX.

❷

BOOTH THEATRE, BROADWAY

"His stamina and sheer physical control in sustaining the illusion of Merrick's distorted figure are remarkable." Rolling Stone

Bowie's only theatrical role was as John Merrick, in *The Elephant Man*. Thorough as ever, Bowie had spent time researching the part, going to view the somewhat macabre moulds made from Merrick's deformed remains in The London Hospital a few weeks previously. Bowie's performance was a critical triumph, but he decided to end his run on January 3rd, 1981. This may simply have been his slightly 'been there, done that, what's new?' nature – but also at the back of his mind may have been the tragic murder of John Lennon. On 8th December, 1980, Lennon had been shot dead by John Chapman in the doorway of the Dakota building. Eerily, Bowie was on Chapman's radar: he had been to see *The Elephant Man* a few days before. Lennon's death was shocking on a personal level – he and Bowie were close friends and collaborators – but it also made Bowie cautious of contact with the general public.

WHERE?
BROADWAY AND W45TH ST,
MIDTOWN,
MANHATTAN.

❸

CHATEAU DU SIGNAL

"There were a lot of people about but it didn't interest me and to be honest I didn't pay much attention." **Duncan (Zowie) on celebrities visiting Bowie at the chateau.**

After his divorce from Angie, David bought the 14–room Chateau du Signal, built for a Russian emigré in 1900, on the edge of the Sauvabelin forest in the hills above Lausanne. Everyone was a little puzzled that, obvious tax (10%) logic aside, Bowie stuck with Switzerland. He did have family reasons – Zowie was at the Commonwealth American School in Vevey, and needed some continuity. David also enjoyed skiing in Gstaad, and he recorded most of *Lodger* at Mountain Studios in Montreux. Claude Nobs, founder of the Montreux Jazz Festival was also a chum. He was later to marry Iman in Lausanne, but she had other ideas about where to live. Switzerland was too quiet, too dull, too square; it had to be NYC. The Bowies put the Chateau up for sale in 1997; it finally sold for 4 million Swiss francs (US$7 million) in 2000.

WHERE?
SAUVABELIN FOREST,
LAUSANNE,
SWITZERLAND.

❹

RAROTONGA

"Bowie has an inner spirit that is indestructible." Nagisa Oshima, director, *Merry Christmas Mr Lawrence*

It was after cult Japanese director Nagisa Oshima had seen Bowie in *The Elephant Man* that he thought Bowie would be perfect for his next film, the story of a Japanese camp guard (played by Ryuichi Sakamoto) during World War II who develops a love/hate obsessive relationship with a stiff upper-lipped, blue-eyed prisoner-of-war, New Zealand major Jack 'Strafer' Celliers (Bowie). Oshima built a replica POW camp, where most of the tense action was filmed, later set against a Sakamoto soundtrack, featuring David Sylvian. Bowie loved doing the movie over a few weeks in September '82, and treated it as a form of relaxation away from his hugely busy, stressful recording and touring life. He completely immersed himself in the role, including its physical hardships. He wasn't doing it for the money, but exploring another strand as a movie actor. Later scenes were filmed in Auckland. It was a cult rather than commercial success.

WHERE?
RAROTONGA,
COOK ISLANDS ARCHIPELAGO.

❺

POWER STATION STUDIOS

"Nile promised him a hit and, as always, Nile delivers." Carlos Alomar

In 1983 Bowie's unerring instinct for change was again to the fore. Free of MainMan at last, he signed a new deal with EMI, reputedly worth $17 million (equivalent to around $45 million today). Change meant a new producer: Tony Visconti was dropped, and Nile Rodgers, from the super-funky Chic, was brought in. "I want a hit", Bowie told him simply. The result was the album *Let's Dance*, the title track of which also became Bowie's biggest hit single. The LP took just 19 days to lay down at Power Station Studios. Off the back of its success, all his other albums started to chart again (10 were in the UK top 100 – a figure only surpassed by Elvis after he died). Bowie was not only now, finally, mega wealthy; he had gone stratospheric.

WHERE?
441 WEST 53RD STREET,
NYC.

❻

CARINDA AND SYDNEY

"My idea was to present an indigenous people in a capitalist, mainly white society."
Bowie on the *Let's Dance* video.

It was typically elliptical of Bowie that he should wish to do the video for what would be his biggest US hit, *Let's Dance*, in the Australian outback. Carinda is a tiny sheep farming outpost, in far north New South Wales – middle of nowhere. Bowie just walked in one day to the only bar in town, with a small crew, who started to film him doing the single on guitar, with a double bass. A few locals, including some Aborigines, joined in as dancing extras. Intercut with shots of an Aboriginal couple visiting the outback, Sydney Harbour Bridge and Sydney Opera House, the video was a statement, allowing Bowie to make a then uncomfortable political point about underprivileged Aborigines. Later in '83 he filmed the *China Girl* video in Sydney Chinatown and on the beach. This starred Bowie and Geeling Ng, a waitress and model with whom Bowie had a brief affair. Bowie loved Australia and Aboriginal culture in particular – he bought a stunning apartment on Elizabeth Bay in Sydney in 1984, and returned every year until he sold it in '94.

WHERE?
BALCONY OF THE ROYAL OPERA HOUSE,
SYDNEY.

SERIOUS MOONLIGHT

Bowie's tour to accompany the mega success of *Let's Dance* kicked off in Brussels on 18th May 1983. After nine European dates, Bowie peeled off to play a one-off date, organised by Steve Wozniak of Apple, in San Bernardino, California. He performed in front of 250,000, for which he received a then world-record $1.5 million. The eight-month long tour was characterised by huge stadiums and, as well as 42 US dates, included 10 in Australia and four in South east Asia, before closing in Hong Kong on 8th December.

2

NORTH AMERICAN LEG
1983
11 July–17 Sept
42 dates, including Quebec, Montreal, New York, Detroit, Chicago, Vancouver, L.A., Dallas, Austin, Washington DC, Toronto, Buffalo and San Francisco.

1

EUROPE LEG
1983
18 May–30 June
31 dates, including
Brussels, Frankfurt,
Munich, London, Paris,
Gothenberg, West
Berlin, Rotterdam and
Edinburgh. Bowie broke
off mid-way for a festival
in San Bernardino,
California.

3

JAPAN LEG
1983
20–31 Oct
10 dates, including
Tokyo, Yokohama, Osaka,
Nagoya and Kyoto.

5

SE ASIA LEG
1983
3–8 Dec
4 dates, including
Singapore, Bangkok and
Hong Kong.

4

OZ/NZ LEG
1983
4–26 Nov
10 dates, including Perth,
Adelaide, Melbourne,
Brisbane, Sydney,
Wellington and Auckland.

❼

MUSTIQUE

"You'd never know who you would end up meeting when you were on holiday with David." **George Underwood**

David first went to Mustique at the invitation of Mick Jagger and Jerry Hall. He started building his own house on the tiny Caribbean island in 1989, having spotted a six acre plot next to architect Arne Hasselqvist's house. It overlooked Britannia Bay, with the world-famous Basil's Bar at one end. Bowie commissioned Arne, who had also built Mick's and Princess Margaret's houses, together with designer Robert J. Litwiller, to create a house in Balinese, with a touch of British colonial, style. He loved going to Mustique over Christmas, and hanging out at Basil's, often getting up on stage for some impromptu singing. When he met Iman, they would throw one big party a year at the house, including one 70s themed glam rock New Year's Eve party. For David, Mustique was the perfect escape.

WHERE?
BRITTANIA BAY,
MUSTIQUE,
ST VINCENT AND THE GRENADINES,
WEST INDIES.

SEPT '91
TIN MACHINE 2

JULY '92
OY VEY, BABY

APR '93
BLACK TIE, WHITE
NOISE

NOV '93
BUDDHA OF
SUBURBIA

SEPT '95
1. OUTSIDE

1990-2004

The start of 1990 was, more or less, business as usual. Bowie had
decided on a tour to keep his own brand alive, creating some confusion
with his Tin Machine persona. The punishing schedule of the Sound
and Vision Tour kicked off in Quebec in March '90 and ended 6 months
later on 29th September in Buenos Aires. Then in October, everything
changed. He met supermodel Iman and, for the first time, he fell
properly in love. He and Iman married in April '92. The Tin Machine
project had kept going for two more albums, *Tin Machine II* and *Tin
Machine Live: Oy Vey, Baby*. Both marked a bit of a nadir in Bowie's
creative fortunes. EMI dropped Bowie when they heard *Tin Machine
II*, and *Oy Vey* lived up to its name – it was universally panned. Bowie
treated the critical reaction as a kind of purge: having become invisible,
having hit rock bottom creatively, he could restart with a clean slate.
His stock had in any case started to rise. Several new hot bands
on the scene, notably Suede, were emerging, citing Bowie as their
major influence. In '93 he released *Black Tie White Noise*, which went
to Number 1 in the UK (although it failed to chart in the US – largely
the result of his record company's collapse). 1996 saw the release

FEB '97
EARTHLING

OCT '99
'HOURS...'

JUNE '02
HEATHEN

SEPT '03
REALITY

of *Basquiat*, in which Bowie played Andy Warhol. There was also innovation on all sorts of other fronts. Bowie and Iman moved to New York permanently and Bowie returned to painting, and started collecting art seriously. In 1997 he celebrated his 50th and launched Bowie Bonds – investors punted a huge $55 million up front in exchange for a guaranteed return on his royalties from his back catalogue for 10 years. He spent the money on art, buying back the rights (for a reputed US$27 million) to his songs that Defries still held, and on a new interest: the Internet. Bowie was fascinated by the implications of the medium, which he thought would change everything. He even launched his own ISP, BowieNet, in 1998, and developed a reputation as a bit of a futurologist: as early as 2002 he stated that music would be 'like running water'. Bowie released the albums *1. Outside*, *Earthling* and *'hours...'*. 2000 saw his triumphant return to Glastonbury. In 2001, following 9/11 he performed at The Concert for New York City. 2003 was to see David launching his biggest tour for five years, in support of his *Reality* album. After 114 gruelling shows across four continents, the tour was dramatically cut short. Bowie would never tour again.

1

PARIS

"Marrying my wife. That's the most successful thing I ever did in my life... Nothing else counts." **David Bowie**

Bowie had apparently first spotted Iman on the pages of a fashion magazine, whilst on a flight (he had swallowed some of his fear of flying). Born Zara Mohamed Abdulmajid, she was at that point a top fashion model working in NYC. Something was resolved in David's life – he'd had his fill of groupies and mindless sex, he'd had the relationship with someone too young (Melissa Hurley – they were briefly engaged) and Iman just clicked when they finally met at a dinner party thrown by his hairdresser in L.A. in 1990. David proposed, in Paris, along the Seine, in October 1991. They married in secret in Lausanne in April 1992, with a public ceremony at the American Church in Florence two months later, for which Bowie composed much of the music. They had just 68 family and friends at the reception in a former Medici villa, including Brian Eno, Bono and Yoko Ono. Joey (Zowie) was best man.

WHERE?
RIVER SEINE,
BY L'ÎLE DE LA CITÉ,
PARIS.

②

GUGGING

"His gift for the charismatically disturbing seems to have reasserted itself."
Charles Shaar Murray in *The Daily Telegraph*, on *1. Outside*.

It may have been coincidence, but marriage to Iman saw Bowie's creativity revitalised. After *Black Tie White Noise* and *Buddha of Suburbia*, Bowie teamed up again with Brian Eno, with whom he shared a fascination with outsider art and, in David's case, given his family history – and in particular the medical history and suicide of his half-brother Terry – psychiatry. They visited this famous institution just outside Vienna, where people with mental disabilities – 'outsider artists' – were given free reign to create, as part of their therapy. The ideas provoked by Gugging fed into their 1995 album project *1. Outside*, a blatantly artistic rather than commercial endeavour. Bowie was once again, subtly, changing his persona, this time into an elite conceptual artist, perfectly capturing a dark, pre-millennial angst.

WHERE?
MARIA GUGGING PSYCHIATRIC CLINIC,
KLOSTERNEUBERG,
NEAR VIENNA,
AUSTRIA.

❸

THE GALLERY

"My art has little to do with trends, and nothing to do with style."
David Bowie

Bowie had been creating art in various media – painting, sculpture and installation – since the early '70s. He was also an avid collector, particularly of German Expressionist painting, contemporary African art, Memphis Group furniture, post-war British sculpture, Basquiat, Patrick Caulfield and Damien Hirst, to name a few. He collaborated with Hirst on one of his 'spin' paintings (*Beautiful, hallo, space-boy painting*, of 1995). He also joined the editorial board of *Modern Painters* magazine, for which he interviewed Balthus, Tracey Emin, Jeff Koons and Hirst. It was a brave move to take the plunge and hold an exhibition of his own work, in London's Cork Street, in April 1995. He showed works inspired by the Minotaur of Knossos (with big cock and balls), his Hirst picture, *Ancestor* – a work inspired by a trip to South Africa with Iman – and a chrome Aladdin Sane mask. Bowie had already crossed from music to film effortlessly; the show revealed how he could do the same with art.

WHERE?
THE GALLERY,
CORK STREET,
MAYFAIR,
LONDON W1.

❹

BASQUIAT

"The first film [by a painter] about an American painter, and it's a black painter,"
David Bowie in *Ikon*.

It was somehow very fitting that Bowie should star in painter Julian Schnabel's first movie, about New York graffiti artist, Basquiat, who died of a heroin and cocaine overdose in 1988, aged 27. Bowie was now deep into the modern art scene, was completely across the febrile, fickle nature of the gallery/artist relationship, and he got to play one of his early icons, Andy Warhol, wearing some of Andy's original clothes and his actual wig. "They still smelt of him," he was quoted as saying, rather eerily. The result divided opinion. David Bailey thought it was awful, with Bowie playing Warhol as way too camp, others called it Bowie's best film performance. Paul Morrissey, director of many Warhol's movies, thought Bowie's depiction of the artist was the best on film: "Bowie at least knew Andy. They went to the same parties."

5

285 LAFAYETTE STREET

"I can't imagine living anywhere else. I've lived in New York longer than I've lived anywhere else. It's amazing. I am a New Yorker." Bowie, interviewed in 2003.

David and Iman first lived together in New York in a condo on 708 Broadway. Then in 1999 they bought two apartments at the top of this building to create a vast penthouse, with 26-foot high ceilings, wood burning fireplaces and a roof garden. The location was typically Bowie – away from the fray for being high up, but also close to all the things he loved about NYC – Greenwich Village, the Strand Bookstore, SoHo, Dean & DeLuca deli, Bleecker Bob's record store, McNally Jackson Books, Caffe Reggio and Washington Square Park. Bowie was quite happy to walk the streets, pretty much like any other local, with Iman and daughter Lexi, and, unlike London or Paris, he wouldn't be bothered: "It's so easy to be a person here, a regular guy."

WHERE?
285 LAFAYETTE STREET,
SOHO,
NYC.

BOWIE IN MANHATTAN

Bowie loved New York, was at ease there and in later years considered himself a New Yorker above anything else. When he and Iman bought their apartment on Lafayette in 1999, they weren't just buying an amazing property, but moving into a neighborhood. Here he, Iman and Lexi could live in relative anonymity, popping into favourite cafes, bookshops and delis. Like any other New Yorker he rode the subway, hailed cabs or simply walked, without any minders. Unlike London, New York didn't suffer from celebrity-chasing bullshit. By all accounts, he and Iman were intensely happy living a family life in NYC.

❶ *Bleecker Bob's*
Bowie loved shopping for rare vinyl here. It sadly closed in 2013, to make way for a frozen yogurt outlet.

❷ *The Strand bookstore*
Bowie loved browsing in this huge, wonderfully traditional bookshop. He was quoted as saying "It's impossible to find the book you want, but you always find the book you didn't know you wanted."

❸ *McNally Jackson Books*
Another of Bowie's independent bookshop haunts. A tweet by the bookshop after Bowie's death said "We were lucky enough to occasionally get to sell books to David Bowie. who, in addition to being, you know, Bowie, was also a great reader."

❹ *Washington Square Park*
10 minutes from 285 Lafayette Street, Bowie loved an early morning walk here. He once described it as his favourite place in NYC.

❺ *Caffe Reggio*
This coffee shop was founded in 1927. Bowie was a regular for breakfast or coffee.

❻ *Olive's*
This deli was a favourite, and a chicken and watercress with tomatoes sandwich his regular order.

❼ *Bottega Falai*
Very close to his apartment, Bowie was here very frequently. The prosciutto and watercress sandwich was a favourite.

❽ *Dean and DeLuca*
The very fashionable deli – an institution in NYC – was where Bowie enjoyed shopping for groceries, once a week when he was in town.

❾ *285 Lafayette Street*
The two penthouse apartments which Bowie and Iman bought in 1999 and knocked into one. It was here, surrounded by family, that he died in January 2016.

❿ *New York Theater Workshop*
Where Bowie worked on the musical *Lazarus* shortly before his death.

⓫ *Crosby Street Hotel*
Bowie and Iman frequently attended events here. It was conveniently close to home.

⓬ *The Magic Shop*
The studio where Bowie secretly recorded his album *The Next Day*.

⬤ *Ludlow Street*
Location of three innovative music venues: Pianos, The Living Room and Cakeshop. Bowie would occasionally drop in.

❻

GLASTONBURY

*"He finished up with an encore of **Heroes**, which is the best song in the world as far as I'm concerned."* **Michael Eavis**

You're Michael Eavis, you're organising the millennium Glastonbury, you need the most iconic star since the festival started; who do you call? Bowie had Eavis on the 'phone the Christmas before, 29 years after he had first played at dawn on the Pyramid Stage in 1971. This was going to be a retrospective, the first greatest hits show for a decade. And the set list didn't disappoint old fans or new: it included *China Girl*, *Changes*, *Life on Mars*, *Absolute Beginners*, *Ashes to Ashes*, *Rebel Rebel*, *Golden Years*, *Fame*, *All the Young Dudes*, *Station to Station* and *Under Pressure*. If some worried that critical songs were missing, they needn't: *Ziggy Stardust*, *Heroes*, *Let's Dance* and *I'm Afraid of Americans* made up the encore. Bowie looked amazing in an embroidered frock coat. 100,000 attended (not including gatecrashers). It was a triumph. To cap an amazing year, his daughter Alexandria was born in August, and an NME musicians' poll hailed Bowie as the most inspiring influential artist of all time, ahead of Radiohead and The Beatles.

WHERE?
WORTHY FARM,
PILTON,
SOMERSET.

118

7

LITTLE TONCHE MOUNTAIN

"It's stark, and it has a Spartan quality about it." Bowie, in *The Telegraph*.

When David and producer Tony Visconti went to cut his new album, *Heathen*, in 2001, they chose Allaire Studios, in Shokan, Ulster County – two hours drive from Manhattan, in the Catskills near Woodstock. David fell in love with the landscape and the slightly Spartan quality of Ulster County, and he and Iman bought a 60-acre wooded plot on Little Tonche Mountain, where they built a house in part inspired by his house in Mustique. The purchase and location, made through an LLC rather than in their own names, were closely guarded secrets. David could breathe up here, driving around the empty country lanes in his two-seater convertible Mustang. So close to NYC, but yet so far.

WHERE?
LITTLE TONCHE MOUNTAIN,
SHOKAN,
OLIVE,
ULSTER COUNTY.

❽
MADISON SQUARE GARDEN

"I didn't want to open with a celebratory mood. We were all devastated." David Bowie

When 9/11 happened, on that fateful, clear September morning, Bowie and Visconti were still at Allaire Studios. Iman was in the City, in the Lafayette Street apartment, just a few blocks north of the World Trade Center. David managed a short conversation with her before phone communications were cut off. The next 24 hours were ones of extreme worry. Just over a month later, David opened the Concert for New York City, in support of the Robin Hood Foundation, and in honour of the NYC Fire Department, NYPD and all those who lost their lives. David opened with a rendition of Paul Simon's *America*, on a simple Omnichord keyboard, before following with a hugely emotive and rousing *Heroes*. David was a self-declared New Yorker, and he felt the impact of 9/11 deeply; he spoke of the sense of loss he, Iman and Lexi felt everytime they walked past their local fire station, just one and a half blocks from home.

WHERE IS IT?
MADISON SQUARE GARDEN,
PENNSYLVANIA PLAZA,
NYC.

REALITY TOUR

Bowie launched *Reality* with a digital broadcast of a performance of the album to 68 cinemas in 22 countries. He kicked off the tour proper on 7th October, 2003 in Copenhagen. After 32 European shows, the US leg opened in Atlantic City, before going onto New Zealand and Australia in February 2004. After a South east Asian leg, he was back in the US at the end of April, with a further 39 US/ Canada dates, before returning to Europe on June 11th. Bowie was having fun, but it was a punishing schedule, not least for a 57-year old.The final show of the tour took place at Scheessel in Germany. just 14 days later, when Bowie was rushed to hospital with a serious heart condition. The final 11 planned shows were cancelled. Bowie would never tour again.

②
NORTH AMERICAN FIRST LEG
2004
6 Dec 2003–7 Feb 2004
First 5 dates cancelled due to illness. 20 dates including Montreal, New York, Cleveland, Detroit, Chicago (3 shows), Denver, Calgary, Vancouver, Las Vegas, L.A. and Phoenix.

⑤
NORTH AMERICAN SECOND LEG
2004
29 March–5 June
40 dates (one cancelled), including Philadelphia, Boston, Toronto, Ottawa, Quebec City, Winnipeg, Edmonton, Kelowna, Portland, Seattle, Santa Barbara, L.A., Denver, Austin, Houston, New Orleans, Tampa, Atlanta, Kansas City, Hershey, Washington DC, Pittsburgh, Columbus, Buffalo, Scranton and Atlantic City.

EUROPE FIRST LEG
2003
7 Oct–28 Nov
31 dates, including
Copenhagen, Helsinki,
Stockholm, Hamburg,
Paris, Milan, Zurich,
Munich, Vienna, Cologne,
Berlin, Antwerp, Toulouse,
Manchester, Birmingham,
London.

 EUROPE SECOND LEG
2004
11 June–25 June
7 dates, with a further
14 dates cancelled after
Bowie suffered a heart
attack on stage at the
Hurricane festival in
Scheesel near Hamburg
on 25 June.

❹ **SOUTHEAST ASIA LEG**
2004
4 March–14 March
5 dates, including
Singapore, Tokyo, Osaka,
Hong Kong.

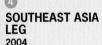 **OZ/NZ LEG**
2004
14 Feb–1 March
7 dates, including
Wellington, Brisbane,
Sydney, Adelaide,
Melbourne and Perth.

9

ST GEORG HOSPITAL, HAMBURG

"I am so pissed off because the last 10 months of this tour have been f******* fantastic." Bowie in *The Daily Telegraph*

There had been intimations of mortality for Bowie on stage on the Prague leg of his *A Reality tour*. After *Reality*, the ninth song, Bowie suddenly left the stage in terrible pain. He returned for *China Girl*, but had to leave two songs later. Back again on stage, he didn't manage to finish *Changes*, the last song of the set, leaving in agony. The world's media were told it was nothing serious, just a pinched nerve. Two days later he was at the Hurricane Festival near Hamburg, but straight after the concert he was rushed to the St Georg Hospital in Hamburg, where he was diagnosed with an acutely blocked artery and underwent an angioplasty. The rest of the tour was cancelled. Bowie's major touring days were over. He would never play a major gig again.

WHERE?
A PATIENT UNDERGOING A VERY SIMILAR OPERATION
TO BOWIE'S AT THE ST GEORG HOSPITAL,
LOHMÜHLENSTRASSE,
HAMBURG.

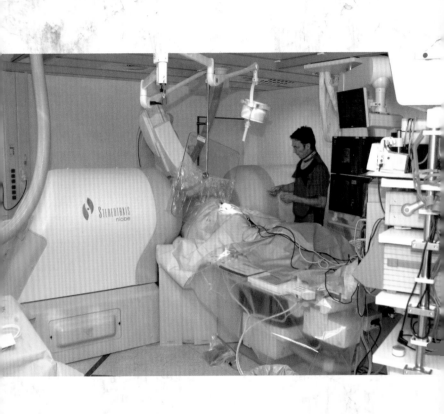

JUNE '07
GLASS SPIDER

JAN '10
A REALITY TOUR

MAR '13
THE NEXT DAY

NOV '14
NOTHING HAS
CHANGED

SEPT'15
FIVE YEARS

BOWING OUT

"The greatest comeback in history."
The Independent

If Bowie would never tour again, he was still writing and recording. He did appear on stage, at a Fashion Rocks benefit for Hurricane Katrina victims in 2005, but his voice was noticeably diminished. In 2006 there was a brief appearance at London's Albert Hall at a Syd Barrett (Pink Floyd) tribute concert. In 2009 he showed up at the Sundance Film Festival. David Bowie was becoming a recluse. Then, out of the blue, on 8th January 2013, *Where are We Now* was released, no fanfare, no PR, no marketing, just a grainy video. Bowie fans worldwide went nuts, and the single shot to the top of the download charts. In March the album, *The Next Day*, went straight to Number 2 in the US and Number 1 in the UK. In March 2013, the London V&A exhibition *David Bowie Is* opened, and broke all attendance records. Bowie's presence was suddenly felt everywhere, as though he hadn't been away.

JAN '16
BLACKSTAR

Then in November 2014, Bowie was diagnosed with liver cancer, with a terminal prognosis. Rather than just fade, he took this as a spur to create again, this time wrapping his music and his imminent death inextricably as one work of art.

①

DAVID BOWIE IS

"I think he was genuinely interested in what someone else might make of it all."
Curator, Victoria and Albert Museum

The most successful exhibition in the 164-year history of the V&A, opened its doors on 22nd March 2013. Bowie allowed Geoffrey Marsh, the curator of the show, full access to his archive, archived so precisely as though, subliminally, he was anticipating it. Over 300 objects featured. The only object which Bowie didn't surrender was the bakelite Grafton sax which Haywood Jones, his dad, had given him for his 13th birthday. Bowie declined to talk to the V&A – it had to be their take on his life and work. Bowie, Iman and Lexi were in London for a secret preview; they spent an hour and a half going round. Later on that same trip they would visit his childhood homes in Brixton and Bromley. 312,000 saw the show in London, before it went on tour to Toronto, Sao Paulo, Berlin, Chicago, Paris, Melbourne, Groningen, Tokyo and Barcelona by which time it had been visited by 1.5 million more. In March 2018 it opened at the Brooklyn Museum, NYC.

WHERE?
VICTORIA AND ALBERT MUSEUM,
EXHIBITION ROAD,
SOUTH KENSINGTON,
LONDON.

②

BLACKSTAR

"His death was no different from his life –
a work of Art. He made **Blackstar** *for us,*
his parting gift." **Tony Visconti**

Bowie made his death an artwork on the mortality we all share. He began the sessions for *Blackstar* in January 2015 followed by work on the musical *Lazarus* – named after the man Jesus raised from the dead with the words "I am the resurrection" – with rehearsals that September. *Blackstar* is full of allusion, not least the connection with *Space Oddity* and, in astrophysics, the term for the transitional phase between a collapsed star and a state of infinite value. There was also an Elvis song, which Bowie would have known, with the lyric "When a man sees a black star, he knows his time...has come." Poignantly, *Blackstar* was the first Bowie album not to feature his image on the cover. It was released on 8th January 2016, on his 69th birthday. Two days later, Bowie's death was announced in a simple statement posted on his social media accounts: "January 10 2016 – David Bowie died peacefully today surrounded by his family after a courageous 18 month battle with cancer." A more moving, memorable, elegant and deeply thought-provoking ending is hard to imagine. Pure Bowie to the last.

WHERE?
SOMEWHERE IN SPACE.

❸

BRIXTON

"Right now, it feels as if the solar system is off its axis, as if one of our main planetary anchors has lost its orbit." **Michael Stipe, R.E.M.**

Created by Australian artist, Jimmy C, opposite Brixton tube station, in 2013, this mural of Bowie as Aladdin Sane became the scene of an outpouring of grief as the news of Bowie's death on 10th January 2016 broke. By evening, the pavement in front of the artwork was covered in flowers and messages, all revealing how much Bowie's music meant to four decades' worth of fans. That evening crowds, numbering several thousand, gathered and broke into impromptu singing, of *Space Oddity*, *Jean Genie*, *Let's Dance*, and played his music. Shrines sprang up and vigils were held around the world – also in London, in Heddon Street, scene of the iconic Ziggy Stardust cover; in New York, outside his apartment building on Lafayette; in L.A. by his star on the Hollywood Walk of fame; in Berlin outside 155 Hauptstrasse. A year later, the Brixton artwork was protected by Lambeth council and even now, several years on, fans from all over the world come to pay their respects. David Bowie is.

WHERE?
SIDE OF MORLEY'S DEPARTMENT STORE,
TUNSTALL ROAD,
BRIXTON,
LONDON SW9.

CREDITS

Photo credits below are listed in section and page title order. Graffito wishes to thank all individuals and picture libraries who helped track down often elusive images. Special thanks to Jonathan Barnbrook for permission to use the moving and mysterious design he created for Bowie, for *Blackstar*. We also extend great thanks to our designer, Karen Wilks.

PHOTO CREDITS

BEGINNINGS
Stansfield Road Ian Castello-Cortes **Plaistow Grove** Ian Castello-Cortes **The Marquee** Getty Images **Foxgrove Road** Ian Castello-Cortes **The Arts Lab** Ian Castello-Cortes **Space Oddity** Courtesy of NASA **Haddon Hall** Rex Features

1970-71 Mr Fish Ian Castello-Cortes **Greenwich Village** Alamy **Sunset Strip** Rex Features **Glastonbury** Getty Images **The Roundhouse** Getty Images **The Warwick** Alamy **The Factory** Alamy **Studio 54** Rex Features **Max's Kansas City** Rex Features

1972-1973 Friars Aylesbury Rex Features **QE2** Rex Features **Carnegie Hall** Alamy **Tokyo Imperial Hotel** Anton Smith **Trans-Siberian** Alamy **Hammersmith Odeon** Rex Features

1974-1975 Oakley Street Ian Castello-Cortes **Charing Cross Road** Rex Features **Montreal Forum** Alamy **Sigma Sounds** Courtesy of Joel Francis **The Pierre** Alamy **Doheney Drive** Courtesy of Paul Wright **Lake Fenton** Rex Features

1976-1979 Clos des Mesanges Vintage postcard **Chateau D'Herouville** Vintage Postcard **155 Haupstrasse** Alamy **Hansa Studios** Courtesy of Marion Prinz, Edition Intro Meisel Gmbh **Chez Romy Haag** Alamy **Helsinki** Rex Features

1980-1989 Pett Level Ian Castello-Cortes **Booth Theatre** Rex Features **Chateau du Signal** Courtesy Mme B. Cendrars **Power Station** Harry Verde **Rarotonga** Rex Features **Carinda/Sydney** Rex Features **Mustique** Rex Features

1990-2004 Paris Rex Features **Gugging** Getty Images **The Gallery** Rex Features **Basquiat** Rex Features **285 Lafayette** Ian Castello-Cortes **Glastonbury** Rex Features **Little Tonche** Rex Features **Madison Square Garden** Rex Features **St Georg Hospital** Rex Features

BOWING OUT David Bowie Is Rex Features **Blackstar** Courtesy of Jonathan Barnbrook **Brixton** Rex Features

All maps: Karen Wilks.

First published in the United States of America, June 2018.
Gingko Press, Inc. 1321 Fifth Street, Berkeley, CA 94710, USA
First published under license from Graffito Books
ISBN: 978-1-58423-697-9
Printed in China
© Graffito Books Ltd, 2018. www.graffitobooks.com.

Art Director: Karen Wilks
Copy Editor: Serena Pethick
Additional research: Lucy Radford-Earle